Tree Beings

TREE BEINGS

Raymond Huber

Sandra Severgnini

Foreword by
Dr Jane Goodall

First published 2020

Exisle Publishing Pty Ltd
226 High Street, Dunedin, 9016, New Zealand
PO Box 864, Chatswood, NSW 2057, Australia
www.exislepublishing.com

Copyright © 2020 in text: Raymond Huber
Copyright © 2020 in illustrations: Sandra Severgnini

Raymond Huber and Sandra Severgnini assert the moral right to be identified as the creators of this work.

All rights reserved. Except for short extracts for the purpose of review, no part of this book may be reproduced, stored in a retrieval system or transmitted in any form or by any means, whether electronic, mechanical, photocopying, recording or otherwise, without prior written permission from the publisher.

A CiP record for this book is available from the National Library of Australia.

ISBN 978 1 925820 53 9

Designed by Mark Thacker
Typeset in Gimlet Micro Regular 10 on 16pt

Printed in China on 120gsm white wood-free paper

This book uses paper sourced under ISO 14001 guidelines from well-managed forests and other controlled sources.

10 9 8 7 6 5 4 3 2

For my mother, who gave me a love of books, and
my father, who gave me a love of nature.
— R. H.

For Jessica and Tim, whose love of the outdoors
brought them together.
— S. S.

Tree beings are people who love trees:

a young woman who lives high up in a giant tree for two years

a scientist who discovers trees have their own internet

a tree-planter who faces dangers in order to plant trees

young people who fight to save their country's last native forests

a nine-year-old boy who finds a way to plant a trillion trees

… and more.

Discover the power of trees …

There are four big ideas in this book. The first is that trees give life to the planet; the second is that trees can help us fight climate change; the third idea is that trees are like beings; and the fourth is that trees need our help and protection.

Throughout the book you will see words that appear in **green**. If you don't know what the word means, you can look it up in the glossary, on p. 92, where these words are explained.

A message from Dr Jane Goodall — 10

BIG IDEA 1:
Life in the trees

Living up a tree: Julia Butterfly Hill — 14
Green skin of the Earth: How trees give life — 18
Living in the jungle: Dr Jane Goodall — 23
World record trees — 28

BIG IDEA 2:
Trees can save us

Mother of the trees: Professor Wangari Maathai — 32
Powered by trees: Richard St. Barbe Baker — 38
Plant a tree: Save the planet — 42
Trillion tree kid: Felix Finkbeiner — 44
The forest maker: Tony Rinaudo — 49

BIG IDEA 3:
Trees are like beings

Green beings of the Earth — 54
Voice of the trees: Professor Suzanne Simard — 58
Make friends with a tree — 62
The tree climber: Professor Nalini Nadkarni — 64
Spirit of the forest: Trees in human culture — 68

BIG IDEA 4:
Trees need our help

Saving the oldest forest: John Seed — 74
Green warriors of the Earth: The toughest trees — 78
Letter from a tree: Dean Baigent-Mercer — 82
Chipko! The first tree-huggers — 87
What can you do? — 90
Glossary: Science words explained — 92
References — 93
Puzzles & mazes — 94
Index — 95

A message from Dr Jane Goodall

Founder of the Jane Goodall Institute and UN Messenger of Peace

I love the title of this book: *Tree Beings*. I am always being asked to write forewords for people's books, and often must say 'no'. But I cannot resist the opportunity to endorse the book of a person who feels about trees as I do!

Ever since I was a child I have loved trees. The trees in our garden all had names and personalities. I did not think of them as **inanimate** objects, but as living beings. I had a special tree in our garden, a beech tree, up whom I used to spend hours. I named him — not very imaginatively — Beech! I read books up there, or I just sat, feeling somehow closer to the birds and nature. When I began my chimpanzee study in Gombe National Park, Tanzania, one of the things I loved was being able to spend hours in the rainforest while watching or waiting for the chimpanzees. I got to know individual trees and would greet them whenever I passed, pausing to feel the bark. If I pressed my ear to their trunks I sometimes seemed to hear the sap rising to the rustling leaves above. My special tree beings. And when I was deep in the forest I knew a sense of peace and felt a strong spiritual connection with nature. It was from the forest that I learned how everything is interconnected, and how each species of plant and animal has a role to play in the rich tapestry of life.

In this book, Raymond Huber shares with us the inspiring

stories of some very special people who have not only raised awareness about the importance of trees and forests, but fought to save them from loggers and developers. Richard St. Barbe Baker was way ahead of his time, and was responsible for planting more trees than maybe any other single person. He has long been a personal hero of mine, as have John Seed and Wangari Maathai, both of whom took on the fight to protect forests. I also met Julia Butterfly Hill, who spent almost two years up a giant redwood tree (whom she called 'Luna') to protect her from loggers. Then there is Felix. When he was nine years old he started a campaign urging other children to plant millions of trees. He is a perfect example of today's children, who are beginning to understand the importance of trees for the health of planet Earth, and therefore our own health. Many of the members of the Jane Goodall Institute's Roots & Shoots program for young people are choosing to plant trees ... hundreds of thousands of trees every year.

One very exciting story is the discovery by Professor Suzanne Simard. She has shown, through careful scientific research, that trees communicate through the fungi attached to their roots underground. Imagine, some trees can feed their offspring, and even help other trees. In fact, trees *talk* to each other! If you don't know about all this, you will be amazed — there's a treat in store for you, and you'll think about forests in a new way.

As you will read, forests are one of the most important **ecosystems** on Earth, providing us with clean water and air, removing **carbon dioxide (CO_2)** from the atmosphere and breathing out **oxygen (O_2)**. When we destroy forests, huge amounts of CO_2 are released, mingling with the CO_2 generated by our reckless burning of fossil fuels. Therefore, protecting and restoring forests is a really important way of slowing down **climate change**.

Once you realize how trees bring healing and health to the planet you will wonder why we are allowing forests to be destroyed all over the world. I believe the main difference between ourselves and other animals is our highly developed intellect. Next time you look up at the moon in the night sky, just think: 'Wow! Human beings have actually walked up there, all those miles away!' Seeing that we're so clever, how is it possible that we are destroying our only home? I think that too often we do things to make money, or to have an easy life. We don't stop to think about the consequences of our actions. Every time we destroy a forest we are stealing a little bit of our future. And so, I urge you to join the growing number of people who are fighting to protect and restore forests, who are planting and caring for trees.

I hope that many children all over the world will read *Tree Beings* and understand the importance of trees.

Dr Jane Goodall, PhD, DBE

BIG IDEA 1

Life in the trees

Living up a tree

Julia Butterfly Hill

She lived for two years up a massive tree, battered by storms and threatened by chainsaws and helicopters.

When Julia Hill was 22 years old she was badly hurt in a car accident. While she was getting better, she wondered what she would do with her life. Julia and some friends went on a trip to California. They visited a redwood forest where Julia wandered off alone to look at the giant trees. She stopped to gaze up at the ancient redwoods surrounding her. Julia says it was a life-changing moment.

Shortly after, she learned that a **logging** company was cutting down the redwoods. Julia was sickened that trees which had taken thousands of years to grow were now being killed in minutes with chainsaws. Only 5 per cent of the original forest was left.

Julia knew she'd found a new purpose for her life: to save the redwood trees. But not everyone cared that much — even the American President, Ronald Reagan, when asked about saving the redwoods, had said,

'You know, a tree is a tree, how many more do you need to look at?'

Julia joined a protest group trying to stop logging of redwoods. The protestors had forest nicknames, so Julia called herself 'Butterfly' (a name she still has today). One of their protests was called 'tree-sitting': they'd perch high in a redwood, which saved the tree and also got them into the news. But it was dangerous to climb the tallest living things on the planet. Julia was trained in tree-climbing and given the job of sitting up a 60-metre-tall (197-foot) redwood. It was tagged with blue paint, meaning it was soon to be chainsawed down. The protesters had built a platform by moonlight, high in the tree that they named Luna ('moon' in Spanish).

This was the start of a wonderful friendship between a human and a tree. Julia nervously clambered up to the small platform, just 5 metres (16 feet) from the top of Luna. She was shocked to see that the hillside below had already been stripped bare of trees. The loggers now turned towards Luna.

Imagine you are there on that day in 1997...

Far below on the forest floor, Julia hears the waspish buzz of a chainsaw revving up. For a minute she thinks the loggers have come to cut down Luna. But surely they know she's up here, don't they? The threatening saw gets closer and closer. It rises to a screech and chips fly out from Luna's base. When it pauses, Julia calls out, 'Hey! I'm still up here!'

Crack! A branch falls from Luna's base. The loggers are cutting off her lowest limbs. *I won't be scared off so easily*, Julia thinks, more determined than ever to protect Luna.

She watches as the loggers move away. But the chainsaw rattles into life again. They screech again and Julia realizes what's happening. The men are hacking into the trunk of another redwood tree, very close to Luna. As the chainsaw strains, Julia feels as though it is cutting her as well.

The men scuttle away ... Julia looks across at the top of the cut tree ... it sways though there's no wind. A whip crack! And the giant tree begins its descent to the forest floor. Branches explode all around ... whoosh ... boom! Luna shudders.

'Stop!' Julia yells, but her voice is drowned by the machine. Another nearby tree is attacked and cut through. It begins its death dive and it's falling towards Luna. Julia clings on tightly. The massive tree brushes past her with a gust of wind that almost blows Julia off. She hugs the trunk and whispers, 'Thank you, Luna.'

For the start of her tree-sit Julia often had another protester with her, but as winter arrived Julia decided to live there alone. Daily life was tricky up in Luna: toilet waste was stored and later lowered; rainwater was collected for drinking and washing. As time went by Julia tried to talk the loggers below into saving the trees, but many of them just swore at her.

They tried to terrify Julia by buzzing Luna with a helicopter. But she filmed the attack, and the choppers were ordered not to fly so close. The loggers kept her awake at night with air horns and bright lights, but Julia wouldn't budge. Determined to move her from the tree, they blocked her food deliveries. Luna was battered by winter storms and lightning, which shook the little platform. Just as Julia felt herself weakening, some protesters surrounded Luna and sent fresh food up to her.

During one very violent storm Julia was thrown from branch to branch as the treetop waved around. She thought she'd die and cried out for strength. Suddenly it was as if Luna was talking to her, telling her to be like a tree and bend in the wind. Julia let go of her fear and survived the storm.

She'd now been living up in Luna for 100 days and was getting to know the 1000-year-old tree. One day she even felt safe enough to climb barefoot to the top.

Spring arrived and with it came hummingbirds, mice and flying squirrels which raided her food. By now Julia was well known and the world knew about the endangered redwoods because of her. Seasons passed and people gave warm clothes to Julia for her second winter in Luna. But the logging went on in the forest nearby. Helicopters carried off the cut trees, then set fire to the earth. The ground burned for days and Julia felt like she was in a war zone. Redwood bark is up to 30 centimetres (1 foot) thick, which protects it from fire and lightning.

After much talking with the logging company, they finally agreed to protect Luna and a wide area around it. In 1999, Julia touched the earth for the first time in 738 days — a world record for the longest protest tree-sit. Today the trees around Luna are safe, but many other redwood forests are still not protected. Redwoods are the second-biggest living things on the planet (the biggest is a fungus) and they can live to be 3000 years old.

Julia says that living with Luna made her realize that all living things can communicate with us, if we take the time to listen.

Find out more

Circle of Life: www.circleoflife.org
Save the Redwoods League: www.savetheredwoods.org

Green skin of the Earth
How trees give life

Trees are a powerhouse for everything around us: the air, water, soil and wildlife.

Trees pull water out of the ground and send it into the air. The water vapour from forests becomes clouds which make rainfall.

Imagine your bedroom is a mess, a real pigsty, and your parents clean it up for you. Then they leave you a box of chocolates as a gift ... not likely! But trees do just that: they clean up our mess and give us gifts. They lock up our pollution and give us clean air and water, healthy food and soil.

Trees seem to us like silent statues, but look closely and you'll see they're alive with a heartbeat of water, air and living creatures.

Trees eat sunlight

Trees make their own food using a recipe we call **photosynthesis**. Three ingredients — sunlight, air, water — come together in the leaves, which are like the kitchen of a tree. Air is breathed into the leaves and water is sucked up from the soil. The energy of sunlight powers the recipe, mixing the water with carbon dioxide (CO_2) from the air. This makes food for the tree to grow new wood, and there's some leftover oxygen (O_2) that goes back into the air.

Trees breathe

Humans breathe in O_2 and breathe out CO_2. But trees do the opposite: they breathe out O_2, and breathe in CO_2. That's why trees are really important on the planet at the moment – we have too much CO_2!

Trees fight climate change

Trees store carbon — they take the **carbon** part of CO_2 and turn it into wood and leaves. Meanwhile, we humans have made too much CO_2 from our power-plants, cars and planes. This CO_2 gas is trapped in the atmosphere and is making the climate warmer and more extreme. But trees help us repair this mess by sucking up a lot of the CO_2 we make. Forests also keep the air cool, which also helps to fight global warming.

Trees make rain

Not many people know that trees move water around the planet. They pull water out of the ground, draw it up the trunk to the leaves, then the water goes into the air. A large tree can drink hundreds of litres of water a day and pump it into the sky (that's several bathtubs full). This flow of water from forests turns into clouds, which create almost half the world's rainfall. Trees also clean the water that runs through the soil below them.

Trees care for soil

When you look at a tree, you only see half of it. The roots usually cover a much

Some of the carbon released from your first breath on the day you were born is now locked in the wood of a tropical tree.
— Tony Juniper

greater area than the tree above ground. Roots hold the soil together, saving it from being swept away by floods and wind. Forest soil acts like a sponge because it holds water and lets it slowly trickle into streams. Trees are forever building healthy new soil with their fallen leaves and rotting wood.

Trees clean the air

Trees remove air pollution that spews from human cities. A big tree is like a giant air filter, removing about 1 kilogram (2.2 lb) of pollution a year. Trees planted by busy roads are busy cleaning the air for us.

Trees love wildlife

Forests provide homes and food for countless living things. Just one rainforest tree can have about 4000 different species living on it at one time. Even a dead tree is bursting with life — one out of every five animals and plants on Earth needs rotting wood to survive. Swarms of insects, fungi and microbes love to eat wood. And trees feed us with the most delicious healthy foods: fruits, nuts and spices (my favourites are cherries, walnuts and cinnamon!). Trees also give us the gifts of shade and shelter, play and beauty.

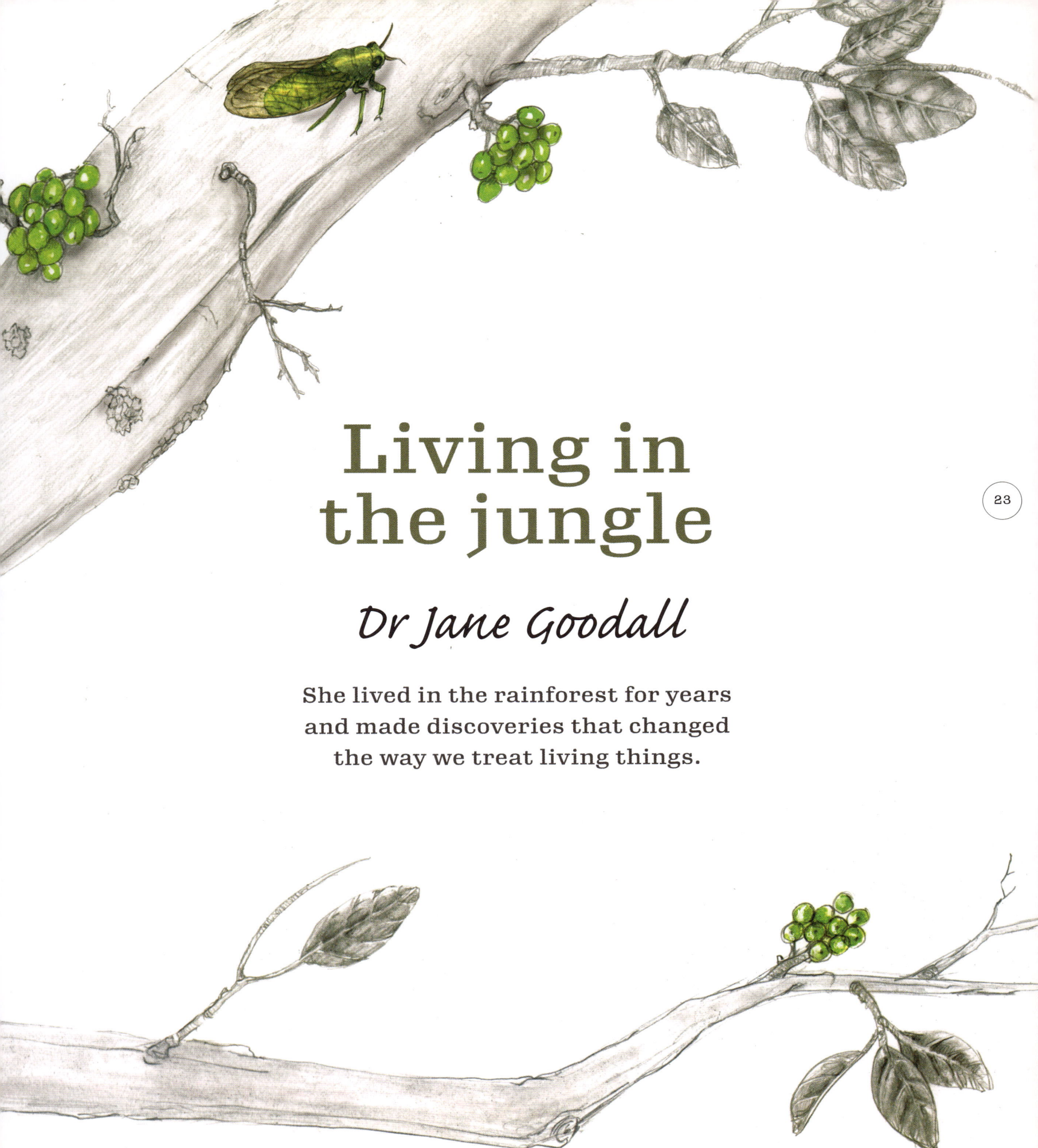

Living in the jungle

Dr Jane Goodall

She lived in the rainforest for years and made discoveries that changed the way we treat living things.

Jane Goodall's love of trees began in her garden. She grew up in England in the 1930s, when children had no TV or computers, so she mostly played outside. She loved the trees that gave her apples and chestnuts, and the trees she'd climb to spy on squirrels and birds.

Jane had a notebook in which she drew plants and animals, and she started a nature club with four friends — later in life she'd start a **conservation** club with hundreds of thousands of young members.

Her favourite was a large tree that Jane called 'Beech'. She'd load a basket with favourite books, a snack and her homework, then climb up Beech and pull the basket up on a string. Her imagination was fed by her reading:

'I would read about Doctor Dolittle and Tarzan and dream about a time when I, too, would live in a forest.'

Beech became like a friend to Jane and during the dark years of the Second World War she would often sit in the tree to be alone and think.

'It was up Beech that I climbed when I was sad, and in the long hours I spent among his branches I came to think of him almost as a person.'

Jane's tree-dreams were the seeds of a plan to go and live in the African jungle. People laughed at her idea of going to Africa, saying that she was 'just a girl' and she should forget that dream. But Jane's mother supported her and Jane held on to her goal. She worked as a waitress to earn money for travel and at the age of 26 she finally made it to Africa. Jane got a job studying chimpanzees in the rainforest at Gombe National Park, Tanzania.

Jane spent years living in Gombe rainforest, much of the time all alone. She

'During all my years in Gombe, I came to realize ... that the forest is a living, breathing entity of intertwining, interdependent life-forms.'

slowly got used to the forest creatures and began to feel that even the trees were beings, like her old friend Beech. Her favourite was a twisted old fig tree which was a **habitat** for many birds and insects, and its fruit attracted chimpanzees. The whole forest was like a community to her and she'd greet the trees and the rivers with a cheerful 'Good morning!'

A rainforest is beautiful, but it also has stinging plants, poisonous snakes and biting insects.

RAINFOREST POWER

Rainforests can actually make it rain! The trees pump so much water into the air that it forms rain clouds. The Amazon is the world's biggest rainforest and it can create its own storms. Rainforests pump out oxygen and fight climate change by soaking up much of our damaging CO_2. Rainforests are also home to over half the world's species of animals and plants. They are a super-power marvel of nature!

Imagine you are there on that day in 1960 …

Jane stretches out on the leaves of the forest floor and gazes up at the canopy of fig trees. Fat cicadas belt out a midday song, blue butterflies dance to their own music, a squirrel capers past, and sunlight plays on every shade of greenery.

Plap! A ripe fig splats on the leaves next to Jane's head. There's a chimpanzee high above her. He ambles through the branches and drops to the ground nearby. Jane knows him well and has named him David Greybeard.

David lies on his back, puts one hand behind his head, looking up at the trees, just like Jane. She dares not move and spoil this magic moment. Suddenly David jumps up and scampers down to the forest creek for a drink. Jane follows.

Jane sits not too far from David at the waterside. She picks up a tasty-looking red fruit and holds it out towards the chimpanzee. David reaches out and takes the gift, then stretches out his hand again and softly holds Jane's hand for a short time. He lets go and walks away into the forest.

Jane sits by the stream in wonder. David is the first chimpanzee to trust her, the strange 'white ape' who's been living in the forest. And now Jane knows for sure that Gombe rainforest is where she is meant to be.

The long lines of army ants were the worst — Jane wouldn't even feel them as they crawled up her leg, then they'd suddenly all bite her at once!

It took many months to get anywhere close to the chimpanzees she was studying, and she sometimes felt it was hopeless. Then at last her patience was rewarded and a big breakthrough came, deep in the forest.

After that, Jane made many new discoveries about chimpanzees. She was the first scientist to watch them using tools and she also showed that they have feelings. Jane's childhood dreams had come true: she was getting to know animals, like Doctor Dolittle, and living alongside them, like Tarzan. Her work gave people a new respect for the lives of creatures living in the rainforest.

By the 1980s she realized that wild animals were vanishing because forests were rapidly being cut down. Jane had to warn the world, so she became a full-time conservationist. For over 30 years now she's travelled the planet fighting for nature. It can be difficult work because of the many threats to the environment, but Jane always carries within her the peace of the forest. She says it was her time living in Gombe rainforest that helps her to keep going.

Jane finds a lot of hope in the energy of young people. She started Roots & Shoots, a club that inspires youth to care for the living planet. Its projects include protecting forests, supporting refugees, and saving animals in many countries. Jane's work with the Gombe rainforest chimpanzees is still going today, making it the longest ever study of animals in the wild.

Find out more

Jane Goodall's Roots & Shoots: www.rootsandshoots.org
The Jane Goodall Institute: janegoodall.org

World record trees

Tallest tree

A redwood tree is the world's tallest living thing at 115.7 metres (378 feet). It's been named Hyperion, after a giant Greek god. The tree grows in California, United States, but the exact spot is kept secret.

Biggest tree

A redwood named General Sherman in California, United States, is the world's biggest tree with a volume around that of ten blue whales.

Oldest tree

The oldest living tree trunk is that of a bristlecone pine, at about 5000 years old, also in California. But the roots of trees can live even longer: the oldest grow under a forest of aspen trees called the 'Pando clone', in Utah, United States … the roots are around 80,000 years old!

Widest tree

A banyan tree (a kind of fig) in the city of Kolkata, India, is the widest on Earth. It covers an area the size of two football fields. The long branches are held up by thousands of **aerial roots** that make the tree look like a forest.

BIG IDEA 2

trees
can *save*
us

Mother of the trees

Professor Wangari Maathai (1940–2011)

She stood up to violent government forces in her work to plant millions of trees.

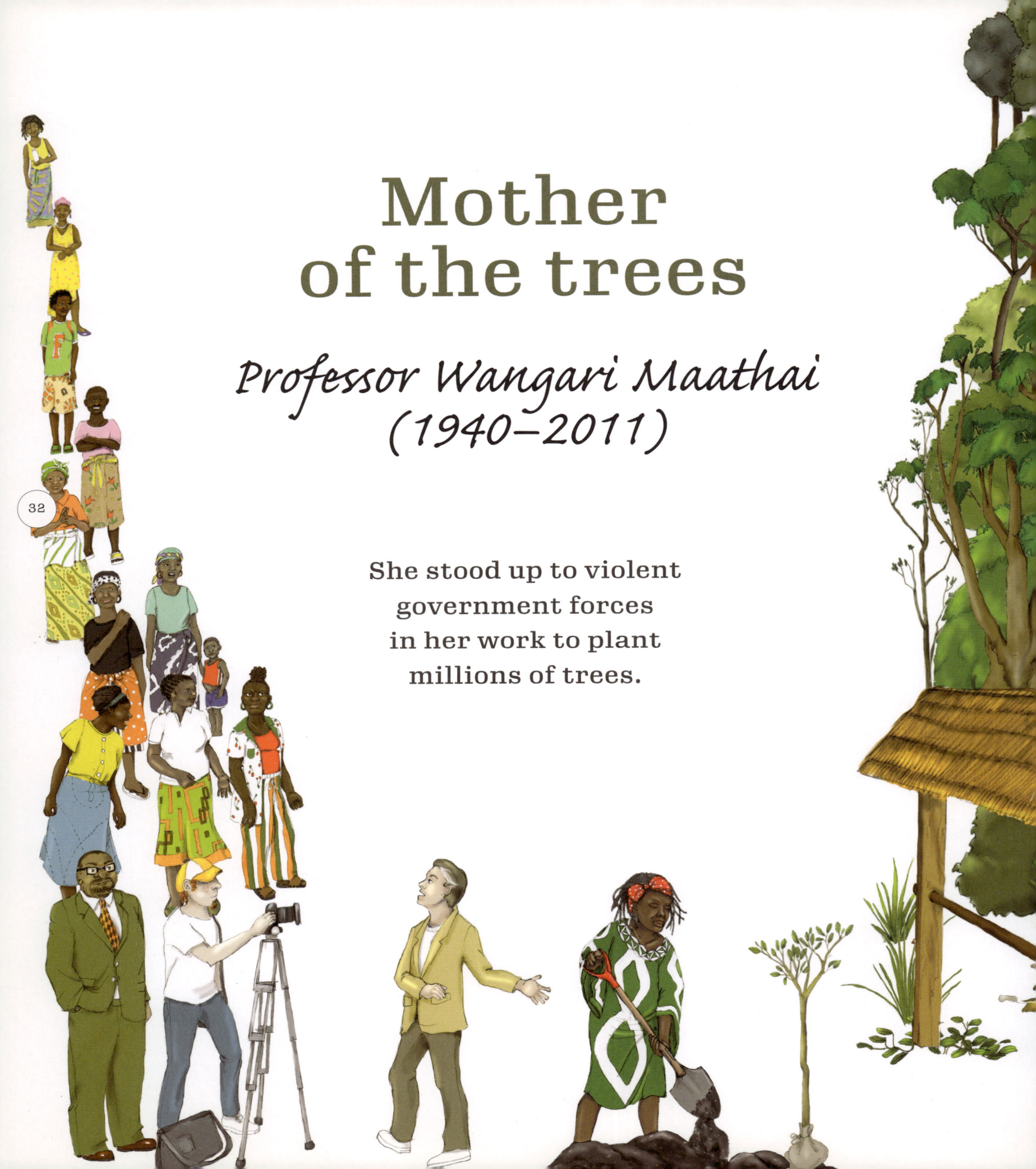

This is the story of girl from a poor village in Kenya, Africa, who became a world leader in tree-planting. When Wangari was growing up, her mother always told her not to fear anything because the name Wangari means 'of the leopard'. Her mother also taught her to care for the massive fig tree in the village, telling her not to cut firewood from the tree. Beside the tree was a stream where Wangari collected water for the family every day. The fig tree protected everything around it. Its roots pulled water up from underground to feed the stream, and the fig's branches were home to many birds and insects. They called the fig a 'tree of God' because it was so helpful.

Most girls in Kenya did not go to school in those days but Wangari's mother sent her anyway. Later, Wangari went to university overseas and became a scientist. But when she returned to her village she was shocked to find the fig tree had been cut down, the stream was dry, and the wildlife was gone. All over Kenya forests had been burned to make way for farms. It soon became harder for poor people to grow food because trees renew the soil and water. Wangari knew she had to do something, and this was her idea: women could plant trees right where they lived.

Wangari started the Green Belt Movement, to plant trees all over Kenya.

Women's groups, schools and churches joined in, planting trees in long rows called 'green belts'. The Movement provided tree **seedlings** and paid people for each tree that survived. Wangari became known as Mama Miti, which means 'Mother of the Trees'.

But Kenya was ruled by a strict government run by President Moi and people lived in fear of his police force. The Green Belt women often protested to

Imagine you are there on that day in 1997 ...

Wangari knows there will be trouble as they walk towards the endangered forest. She expects the police to try and stop them, and she'll never forget the pain of being beaten up. But the protestors have come prepared this time. The Green Belt women have international journalists and politicians marching with them. They've been warned that there is a dangerous gang roaming the forest so they stay outside the main gates to plant a protest tree.

Wangari is starting to dig a hole when out of the forest comes a gang of 200 young men armed with knives and clubs. The men shout and strut about, surrounding Wangari and her group. Some of them are only teenagers.

'You can't enter the forest,' says the leader of the gang. 'Go home, woman!'

Wangari stays as calm as she can: 'I'm not going anywhere until I have planted this small tree.'

'No way,' says the man. 'It's private land.'

'No, it's a public forest,' Wangari says. 'And we have the right to be here.' She keeps digging the hole.

The men yell at her and close in on the group. Suddenly they attack, throwing stones at the unarmed protestors. The women run for their lives, but Wangari is hit on her head. For a moment she freezes in surprise, hardly believing the young men could do this to her. A friend quickly grabs her arm and they escape to their car.

The Green Belt Movement has planted more than 50 million trees around the world.

Fantastic Figs

Fig trees feed more creatures than any other fruit tree in the world. The way they make new fruit is remarkable. There are over 750 different species of fig and each one has a partnership with its own kind of wasp. The tree's flowers are hidden inside its hollow fruit, so it needs help to get the pollen out. A wasp crawls inside the fruit, lays eggs, and then she dies. The tree is now the caregiver of the baby wasps growing inside the fruit! It keeps the fruit warm and protects it with sticky sap. The new wasps exit the fruit covered in pollen, then enter another fruit. The tree gets **pollinated** and the wasp gets a nursery in return.

save trees and President Moi didn't like this. Wangari said in public:

'We have a government in this country that is overseeing the destruction of forests.'

But Moi said Wangari Maathai should be quiet because she was just a woman, and he tried to stop the Green Belt. His government destroyed their tree nurseries and attacked the protestors. Wangari was beaten by police and arrested many times. But like a tree she stood her ground, remembering her mother's words about not being afraid. Wangari needed all her strength to go on because by now she had a family of three children.

The government were going to sell a large forest so the Green Belt led a protest march. They had to stop the forest from being cut down.

Many protestors were injured that day. It turned out the gang had been hired by the police. But thanks to the journalists, the attack was seen on the world news and President Moi was forced to save the forest. Wangari said:

'The government thinks that by threatening me and bashing me they can silence me. But I have an elephant's skin. And somebody must raise their voice.'

Wangari Maathai worked for the Green Belt for 30 years and travelled the world encouraging people to plant trees. At last Kenya got a new government and Wangari was made a Minister for the Environment. Today the Green Belt works in 30 countries, has given jobs to tens of thousands of women, and has planted over 51 million trees.

Wangari was the first African woman to be awarded the Nobel Peace Prize. In her acceptance speech she said:

'I would like to call on young people to commit themselves to activities that contribute toward achieving their long-term dreams. They have the energy and creativity to shape a sustainable future. To the young people I say, you are a gift to your communities and indeed the world. You are our hope and our future.'

'To the young people I say, you are a gift to your communities and indeed the world. You are our hope and our future.'

Find out more

Green Belt Movement: www.greenbeltmovement.org

Powered by trees

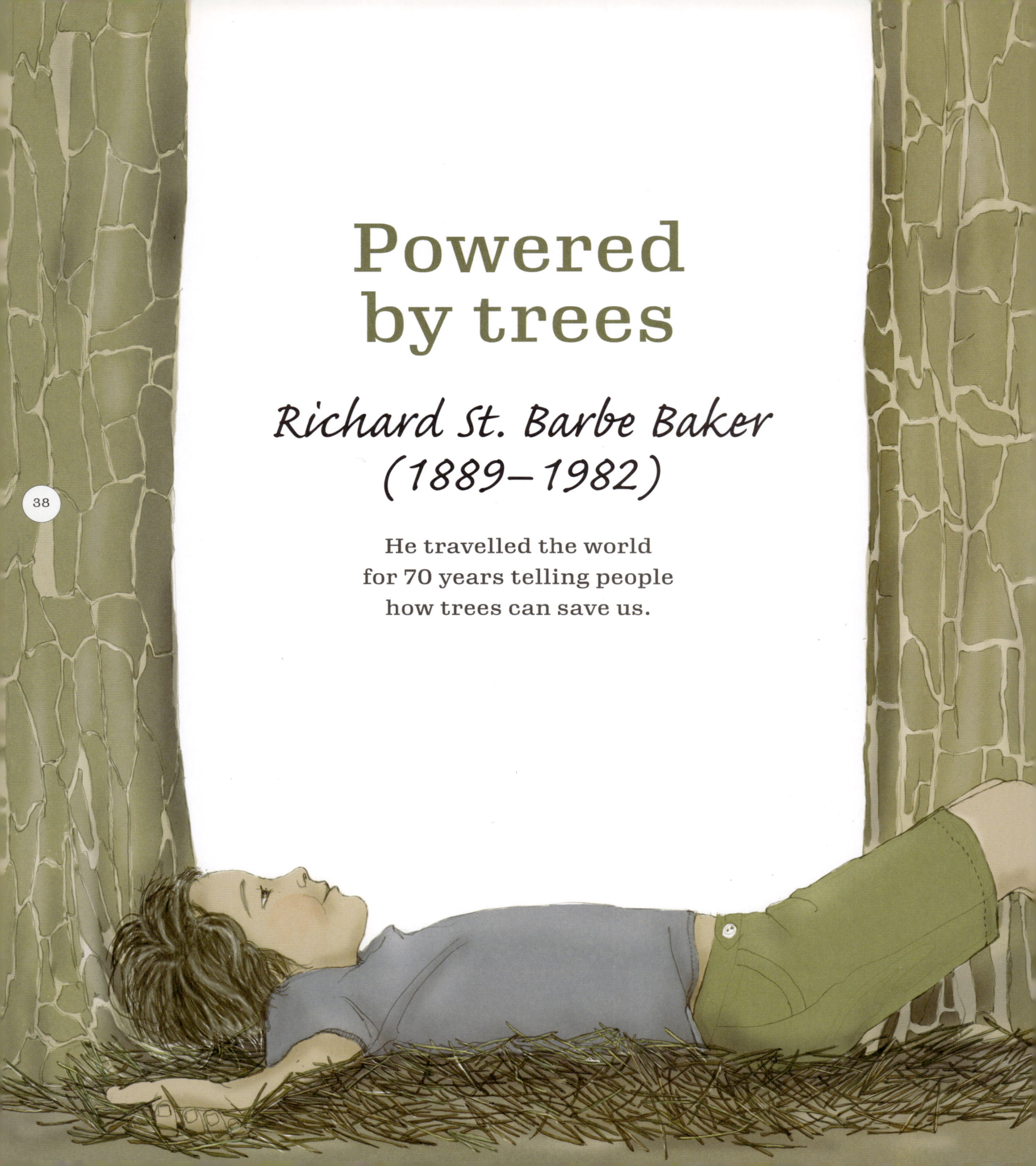

Richard St. Barbe Baker (1889–1982)

He travelled the world for 70 years telling people how trees can save us.

Richard St. Barbe Baker gave his life to trees. It all began in England with an electrifying event when he was five years old. He'd wandered off alone into a pine forest, even though his babysitter had warned him there were snakes and elves in there. Richard got a little lost and walked around in a daydream. He entered a clearing and was stunned by the trees towering over him, beams of sunlight in the mist, and birds singing like a choir. He was so impressed by the beauty of the forest, he lay down on the carpet of pine needles:

'At that moment my heart brimmed over with a sense of unspeakable thankfulness which has followed me through the years.'

While growing up, Richard became friends with an old beech tree near his house. He'd go and visit the tree when he felt unhappy or things had gone wrong at home:

'Standing by the friendly beech, I knew in my heart that my troubles and my grief were but for a passing moment. I would imagine that I had roots digging down deep into Mother Earth and that all above I was sprouting branches. I would hold that in my thoughts for a few moments and then come back with the strength of the tree.'

When he was twenty years old Richard went to Canada, where he had adventures with wild horses and learned a lot from the native Cree people. Richard studied forestry at university and got a job in Kenya, Africa, where he saw that many of the native forests had been cut down. He wanted to help replant the trees so he got to know the local Kikuyu tribes. Dance was important in their culture — they danced for births, deaths and harvests — so Richard suggested they create a new tree-planting dance. But first he had to win the support of the warriors, so Richard organized a Dance of the Trees and invited them. When the day of the dance finally dawned, 3000 warriors were camped outside his hut.

Richard helped the tribes to grow tree **seedlings**, but his British bosses didn't like him getting so friendly with the Kenyans. They destroyed the tribes' nursery of 80,000 trees and replaced it with tennis courts. Then one day, Richard tried to stop a British officer from beating a Kenyan worker. Richard

Richard drove across the Sahara Desert to promote tree-planting.

Imagine you are there on that day in 1922 ...

Richard stands and watches as warriors from many tribes enter the clearing to the beat of drums. Their bodies are painted, decorated with feathers and jewellery, fearsome spears in hand. A huge crowd of spectators follows the warriors as they circle around a lone fig tree. The drumming stops, and Richard's stomach tightens as he finds himself in another electrifying experience. He tells the warriors that trees need their help:

'Listen to me, young men. Your land is turning into a desert. It is time for you to take action. You can become forest planters instead of forest destroyers. Make the trees grow tall once again in your land. Let the war drums beat for the planting of trees!'

The drums begin again, slowly, then faster and faster, now roaring as the warriors dance around the tree. The men stamp and sway, spears thrust upwards, like trees reaching for the sun. From the crowd come young women who form their own circle to dance around the men. The women chant and the warriors answer with an echo.

The dance ends and prizes are given to the dancers. Richard then calls on the dancers to make a three-part promise: to protect their forests; to plant ten trees a year; and to do a good deed every day.

lost his job after that, but he was not put off his tree-quest. He started the first global tree-planting organization, called Men of the Trees, which soon spread to many countries.

Richard pictured the Earth as one great living being, and he knew that trees were connected to everything else: the air, soil, water and wildlife. But humans were removing forests at a rapid speed, so Richard began to travel the world to tell people that we can't survive without trees. He travelled cheaply, working on ships and staying with friends where possible.

Richard was a gifted public speaker and he met with presidents, princes and prime ministers to talk about trees. In Palestine, in 1929, he brought together the leaders of the main religions to plant trees. In 1933 in the United States, he convinced the president to pay unemployed youth to plant billions of trees. Richard also helped to raise about $10 million to save the world's biggest trees, the redwoods.

Richard believed trees are like beings and he said he got energy from trees as he

MAY THE FOREST BE WITH YOU

Forests have a positive 'force' that we humans can sense. Walking in a forest is good for our health — it makes us feel less stressed and it helps us to heal. *Shinrin-yoku* ('forest bathing') is a popular exercise in Japan. It's simple to do *shinrin-yoku*: take a slow walk in a forest with family or friends and enjoy the fresh air and greenery.

got older. He had a habit of placing his hands on a favourite tree trunk for two minutes, both morning and evening.

At 70 years old he rode around England on his white horse, Ghost, telling thousands of school children about trees — the kids called him Ghost Rider. At 74 he rode the whole length of New Zealand on his horse, Rajah, visiting schools on the way. At 88 years old Richard went to the Himalayas to join a protest to save forests (you can read more about this on p. 87).

Richard died aged 92 while on another world tree-planting tour. He'd planted his last tree a few days before, while visiting his old university, in Saskatchewan, Canada. He gave the tree this blessing:

'From our hearts
With our hands
For the Earth
All the world together.'

Richard spent his life speaking for the trees, and as many as 20 trillion trees were planted because of his work. His granddaughter, Ann Marie, says:

'I often wonder what the world would have been like without Grandad; if he didn't inspire thousands of people to plant and protect trees … Imagine if all the armies around the world swapped their guns for spades, and planted trees. This was but one of the many dreams Grandad had.'

Find out more

Richard St. Barbe Baker documentary:
www.nzonscreen.com/title/man-of-the-trees-1981

International Tree Foundation (Men of the Trees):
internationaltreefoundation.org/

Plant a tree
Save the planet

Planting a tree seems like a small thing to do, but it has a big effect — because trees enrich the air, water, soil and wildlife. The CO_2 gas that humans add to the air is warming the planet and making the weather more extreme. The good news is that trees remove CO_2 and slow down climate change. If we planted enough trees it could suck up about two-thirds of the CO_2 we make.

Since humans have been on the Earth we have killed almost half the world's forests. We need to plant more trees, and fast. When you plant a tree it immediately begins to fight climate change. It will also make you aware that you are part of nature.

Ways to plant a tree

Plant a tree in your garden. Choose a tree that's suited to your area — natives are best of all. Plant it where it has room to grow to its full size.

Plant a tree at school. You could even create a mini-forest for your school.

Give a seedling tree as a birthday present for a friend.

Plant a tree in your neighborhood. Join a local tree-planting group.

Plant fruit and nut trees — they'll feed many people for many years.

No birds in your garden? Plant flowering trees to attract birds and insects.

Find out more

Help Plant Trees: www.helpplanttrees.org

The best time to plant a tree was twenty years ago.
The second best time is now.

—Chinese proverb

Trillion tree kid

Felix Finkbeiner

A nine-year-old boy has a plan to
plant a trillion trees to fight climate change ...
and his idea takes off.

Can children save the planet? Yes! said Felix Finkbeiner. He was nine years old when he realized that the future was in the hands of young people.

Felix's adventure began at his school in Germany one day in 2007 when his teacher asked the class to learn about climate change for homework. That weekend, Felix found out that the Earth is warming up because humans are pumping too much CO_2 into the air from power-plants, petrol-powered vehicles, and by burning forests. He thought:

'Our future is being destroyed, and people are just sitting around discussing it. Why haven't we done something!?'

Felix read the inspiring story of tree-planter Wangari Maathai (see p. 32) and he learned that trees soak up CO_2 and cool the air. The solution to climate change jumped out at Felix: the world's children could plant trees wherever they lived.

Felix told his class at school. He called his talk 'The End of the Polar Bears' because they're one of the animals endangered by global warming. He finished his talk by saying:

'Let's plant one million trees in every country on Earth.'

Felix's classmates loved the idea that they could fight climate change by planting trees. He visited other schools and gathered support for his project. All around Germany schools began to plant trees.

Felix had always been an independent child: when he

was only seven he insisted on going to a school of his choice, which meant a long trip alone on public transport. His father said Felix is what Germans call a 'thick wood driller', meaning that he has strong willpower. But Felix knew he couldn't achieve his dream alone — to save the planet, children had to act as a global family. A group of young people worked with Felix to start an organization, and his family also helped. They named themselves Plant-for-the-Planet, and within one year they'd organized the planting of 50,000 trees. Young people everywhere joined the group and planted trees in their own countries.

Plant-for-the-Planet's one millionth tree was planted in 2010, so they set a new target of one trillion trees. They also train young people to spread the word about how trees can slow down climate change. They call them 'Climate Justice Ambassadors' because unfairness is part of the problem. Poor people suffer most from climate change but it's the richer countries that have caused it. A person in a rich country makes about 40 times more CO_2 than a person in a poor country.

Felix met his hero Wangari Maathai and they decided to

WOLVES IN SCOTLAND

Most of Scotland's native forests have gone, which makes the surviving Caledonian forest a very rare place. When the trees were cut down many wonderful animals also disappeared, including lynx, bears and wolves. Volunteer workers have spent the last 30 years saving and restoring the Caledonian forest in Scotland. They've planted over a million new trees and fenced around old trees to stop deer eating seedlings.

The forest is returning, along with the flowers, insects, birds, beavers and squirrels. One day soon there might be wolves again in the forests of Scotland.

'Wangari, you were such an inspiring personality. You will continue to live in thousands of children. We children will fulfil your vision. You will be proud of us while looking down to Earth!'

Plant-for-the-Planet is run by young people and raises money by selling chocolate and T-shirts. Its website records the number of trees planted worldwide. They're on track to reach one trillion trees, which will clean up a huge amount of CO_2 pollution. It will also create 100 million jobs for people who look after the young trees. It's saving the living planet, tree by tree, all because a nine-year-old boy took the future in his hands.

work together. Wangari said that when people join together for a shared goal they can do what might seem impossible. A tree that grows all alone will not last as long as a tree growing within a forest. Felix and Wangari both captured the power of large numbers of people.

When Wangari died, Felix wrote:

The only answer is to plant more trees — to plant trees for our lives.
—Richard St. Barbe Baker

Find out more

Plant-for-the-Planet: www.plant-for-the-planet.org

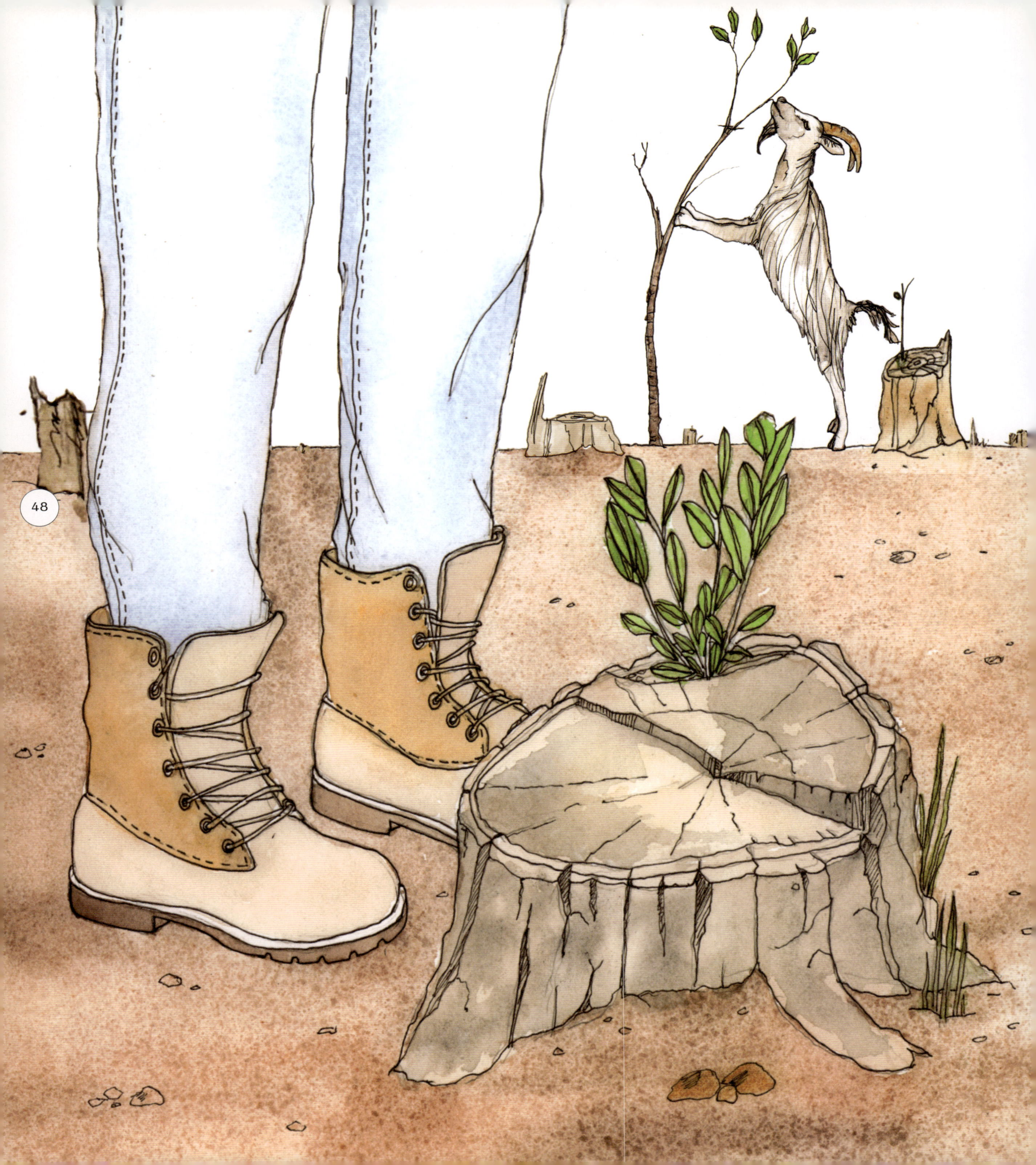

The forest maker

Tony Rinaudo

He discovered a hidden underground forest that stopped a disaster in the desert.

Tony Rinaudo always loved native trees, but he'd seen too many cut down where he grew up in Australia.

Tony prayed that God would help him find a way to help the world's poor. In his early twenties he got a job in Niger, Africa, where people were often starving. Farmers had cut down their trees to make more farmland, so Tony worked with them to plant new trees. But the seedling trees were quickly killed by the heat and dust storms, eaten by goats, or used for firewood. The young Australian began to feel his mission was impossible and he was about to give up.

'When I was a boy, I could not understand why nearly every tree had been removed from farmland and why hills were left bare and eroded, and I was disturbed that children just like me, who through no fault of their own were born in less fortunate countries, were hungry. And I wondered how it could be that these things were accepted as normal.'

One day in 1983, Tony was driving along a sandy road towards a village when he stopped and got out of his Jeep. He looked out at the vast desert, which was dotted with small green bushes. Tony knelt down and looked closely at one of them … he suddenly realized they were not bushes at all … they were trees! The green shoots were growing from old tree stumps. He'd been driving past these bushes for years

Tony chooses the best shoots to grow into tall trees.

without twigging they were really trees. Tony thought to himself, *Even though these trees were cut down long ago, their roots are still alive*. He didn't have to plant new trees at all, they were already there waiting in a kind of underground forest. This was Tony's 'aha!' moment, and it would change the lives of millions of people in Africa.

But why hadn't the stumps already grown back into full-sized trees? Because farmers would cut off the new tree shoots to clear the land every year. Tony showed them how to protect the tree stumps and to make the shoots grow faster. In just a few years they grew back into 5-metre-tall (16-foot) trees.

The trees made the soil better for crops and protected it from wind and floods. Farmers were soon growing twice as much food. After a while the adult trees also gave people fruit, firewood and food for farm animals. They also increased shade, making temperatures about 10 degrees cooler.

Since Tony started his project in Niger, over 200 million trees have been regrown from stumps. His idea of bringing underground forests to life has now spread to many more countries. Tony teaches farmers across the world how to regenerate their trees. They call him The Forest Maker.

Find out more

Right Livelihood Award for Tony: https://www.rightlivelihoodaward.org/laureates/tony-rinaudo/

52

BIG IDEA 3

trees are like *beings*

Green beings of the Earth

Trees are smarter than they look.

It's easy to ignore trees because they don't make a fuss. They stand in the same place and grow so slowly we don't think of them as beings, as we do animals. Yet trees are by far the oldest living things on Earth, and they do have their own kind of intelligence. Trees have no eyes, noses or ears, but they're experts at sensing the area around them.

Trees can send messages to each other through an underground web of fungi.

55

Tree talk

Trees don't have brains, yet they can communicate with each other. One way they do this is by sending chemical messages through the air. Tree leaves can make scents that warn other trees of pest attack. Nearby trees will 'smell' the message with their leaves and start to produce an insect repellent.

Acacia trees in Africa use these airborne scents to protect each other. If a hungry giraffe chews on an acacia tree, the leaves pump out a warning scent, which floats on the breeze to nearby trees. These neighboring trees quickly create an 'anti-giraffe' flavour in their leaves … and the giraffes won't eat them.

Trees can also use airborne messages to ask animals for help. For example, apple trees invaded by caterpillars can produce scents that attract birds to eat the pests. And pine forests attacked by aphids can send out a perfume that brings ladybirds to eat the aphids.

Time telescopes

Because they live for so long, trees can tell us about the distant past. Looking at the rings inside a fallen tree trunk is like looking back in time — each ring shows one year of the tree's growth. Really old tree rings are a record of changes in climate, sometimes going back thousands of years. The rings will be wider in a warm, wet year; and thinner in a cold, dry year. Looking at tree rings is like looking through a 'time telescope'.

Tree internet

Trees also talk to each other under the ground. In many forests they use their roots to keep in touch. They do this with the help of fungi. Tree roots are covered with threads of fungi which reach right inside the roots. Trees and fungi can actually feed each other. Fungi take food and water from the soil and give it to trees — and in return, the trees give the fungi some food. But trees also use the fungi for something more amazing: contacting other trees. A tree can send its own food, water and messages to other trees through the fungi.

Scientists call this friendship between tree roots and fungi the **wood-wide-web** because it's a massive network like the internet. The fungi cover a wide area under a forest, so trees can use it to connect to other far-off trees. For example, a tree might send chemical signals along the fungal web to warn other trees of an insect attack.

Mother trees

Forest trees also use the wood-wide-web to deliver food and water to other trees that are in trouble.

In a beech forest, for example, the trees that have made a lot of food share it with trees that have less food, or are sick. There are special 'mother' trees in a forest, which care for trees around them by using the web. Mother trees can send food and water to small seedlings struggling to grow in the shade. Mother trees are the biggest, oldest trees with the most connections to the wood-wide-web — they're the busiest points on the tree internet. If mother trees are cut down, the whole forest suffers.

This sharing can even happen between different species of tree. And when a tree is dying it will send its food to nearby trees through the web. A forest is really like a community of trees that care for each other.

Tree senses

Trees can't run away or hide, so they use their smart senses to defend themselves from attack. For example, beech trees and maples know when a deer is nibbling their leaves. When they sense the deer's saliva, the trees quickly create a chemical in the leaves that makes them taste horrible to the deer.

Slower, not lower

We humans sometimes think trees are a 'lower' kind of life that's not as smart as us. But growing slower doesn't mean lower. The tree family has been on Earth for 300 million years, the human family for only 0.1 million years. Science has now shown that trees are experts at sensing light, chemicals, electricity, temperature and gravity. Trees are vital for the health of the planet's climate, water, soil and wildlife. They deserve our respect and care.

> ### Find out more
> *Can You Hear the Trees Talking?* by Peter Wohlleben

Voice of the trees

Professor Suzanne Simard

She discovered how trees use a 'wood-wide-web' to talk to each other.

When she was a child, Suzanne Simard spent a lot of time in the beautiful forests of British Columbia, Canada. Her family often had holidays in the forest, along with their dog, Jigs the beagle. Young Suzanne loved to lie on the ground, staring at the treetops, or to study the creatures in the soil — sometimes she'd even taste a bit of the forest floor. One memorable summer's day, nobody in the family noticed when Jigs ran off into the forest.

Imagine you are there on that day ...

Suzanne hears an eerie cry from the forest. *That's Jigs,* she thinks. *But why is his bark so high-pitched and far away? What mischief is he up to?*

'Jigs! Here, Jigsy!' she calls. But the dog's yelping just echoes back from the trees.

Something's wrong with Jigs, Suzanne thinks. The barking is crazy now.

She walks into the forest towards the worried cry. Suzanne suddenly imagines poor Jigs with his foot crushed in a bear trap. The noise leads her straight to the outhouse. The door is open and the howling comes from deep within.

'Please, not that,' says Suzanne. But she knows she must look into that place you never want to look. Sure enough, there is Jigs, at the bottom of the toilet pit.

Someone forgot to latch the door shut. And Jigs loves a nice ripe smell.

Suzanne looks down at Jigs, squirming in the muck below. The pit is narrow with vertical sides — it's too deep for arms to reach the slippery dog.

Before long the whole family has arrived to try and figure out how to save Jigs. They push aside the wooden hut on top and dig the soil away from one side of the pit. At last they reach the stinky dog, who is thrown into the lake for a wash.

But Suzanne goes back to the enlarged hole and is spellbound by what she sees. The digging has uncovered a massive tangle of tree roots set within coloured layers of soil. There are tiny creatures crawling around, and most fascinating of all is the web of white fungi, like tiny wires connecting everything. Suzanne realizes for the first time that there's a whole other world hidden underneath the forest floor. The roots are as full of life as the treetops.

The underground forest continued to interest Suzanne as she got older — it was like a buried treasure waiting to be claimed. To find out more she studied trees at university and then got a job in a forest where trees were being harvested. Suzanne was shocked to see trees being 'clear cut', which meant that every living thing was shaved off the forest floor by logging machines. She realized that trees were just treated as dumb objects with no connection to the rest of nature. But she'd always believed that the trees, animals, fungi and

Trees can share food with each other through the fungi that connects their roots.

insects were like a community — all living things needed each other. Suzanne returned to science, studying trees and fungi in Canada's forests.

Her work wasn't easy, because doing experiments in a living forest had more hazards than in a laboratory — she had to carry sprays to repel both mosquitoes and bears! One day she did an experiment to find out if the underground fungi were connecting the roots of two different kinds of trees, a birch and a fir. As she set up the recording machine, a huge grizzly bear and her cub came ambling towards her. Suzanne ran back to her truck and waited a while until the bears finished feeding, then returned to check the experiment. When she played back the recording, the results amazed her:

'I heard the most beautiful sound. Kkhh! It was the sound of birch talking to fir, and birch was saying, "Hey, can I help you?" And fir was saying, "Yeah, can you send me some of your carbon?"'

The birch tree was sharing its own food (the carbon) with the fir tree by sending it through the web of fungi. It was a life-changing moment for Suzanne:

'I knew I had found something big, something that would change the way we look at how trees interact.'

She studied forests for over twenty years and proved that trees were connected to fungi in order to share food, water and messages. This living internet was named the 'wood-wide-web'.

Suzanne has since started the Mother Tree Project to help protect important trees in Canadian forests. Her work showed that trees can work together and communicate with each other. They are not dumb wooden objects, but beings with their own hidden intelligence.

TREE TALK

Trees have become part of our everyday language:

I'm going out on a limb here,

but am I barking up the wrong tree?

Maybe it's time to turn over a new leaf and branch out a bit.

But I am not out of the woods yet,

I'm stumped by this knotty problem

because I'm as thick as two short planks, and I have a wooden expression,

because I sleep like a log,

which goes against the grain.

The apple doesn't fall far from the tree,

look at my family tree.

That's me, in a nutshell.

Find out more

Suzanne Simard's TED Talk: www.ted.com/talks/suzanne_simard_how_trees_talk_to_each_other

Make friends with a tree

Keep a green tree in your heart and perhaps a singing bird will come.
—Chinese proverb

It would be cool to have a friend like Treebeard in *The Lord of the Rings* — a giant tree to give you rides and talk to you. Treebeard says that trees speak slowly and only when they've got something worth saying.

Making friends with a real tree takes time too, but it's worth the effort. The people in this book had special trees: Jane Goodall named her tree, Richard St. Barbe Baker talked to his, and Suzanne Simard listened to her trees. They all treated trees like living beings. There are over 60,000 different tree species on Earth, and each one has a story to tell.

Here are some ideas for making a tree friend:

Choose a tree you really like and that you see often. Introduce yourself and maybe give the tree a name.

Get to know your tree by looking at it from near and far. Walk around it. What colours, shapes, textures, patterns, light and shade do you see?

Sit or lie beneath the tree and soak in the sounds, the smells and any movement.

What smaller plants and creatures does your tree support? Look very closely at the bark, leaves and flowers.

Visit your tree in all weathers and seasons, in the day and at night. Record what you notice by drawing or writing. You could photograph a branch or leaf several times in one year or for longer.

Read about the science and history of your tree species.

Imagine the roots stretching out underground and think about how the tree connects the earth to the sky. Create some tree art with painting, sculpture, singing, poetry or dancing.

Talk to the tree. Don't be shy; trees are great listeners!

Ask the tree some questions. How long have you been here? What is your life like? What events have happened around you here?

Remember that trees live on a much slower timescale than you. They've been alive longer than any other plants or animals on the planet. It might take a while but you will discover how trees sense the world.

If you ask the tree a question, you may receive an answer, not in the form of a voice, but in what you see or feel or hear.
—Dr Rupert Sheldrake

The tree climber

Professor Nalini Nadkarni

She brings people and trees together through dance, music, art, science and Barbie dolls!

Nalini's great love of trees began when she was a child growing up in Maryland, United States. The driveway of her family home was lined with eight maple trees and every day after school she'd choose one of the trees to climb. Nalini would sit in the limbs of the tree, reading a book and watching the world go by below. She called her favourite maple 'Big Arms' because it had easy-to-climb branches, almost like a ladder to the top. She says:

'That's where it began — I felt safe with this tree, I felt interested in the tree, I'd watch squirrels going back and forth, and the seasons would change … It was then I decided that I wanted to do something in my life that involved trees.'

Her father built a boat-shaped treehouse and Nalini would sometimes sleep the night in it. When she was only nine, Nalini wrote a book about how to climb a tree. She dreamed of finding a job that involved tree-climbing. But did such a thing exist?

Nalini went to university and became a tree scientist. Her first job was in the forests of Papua New Guinea where she studied life in the 'canopy' layer (the treetops) of the rainforest. It was a tree-climbing job! While living there, Nalini was bitten by a mosquito and became sick with malaria — but she got

Nalini's Ship

Trees provide a home for smaller plants such as orchids and ferns.

better with the help of quinine, a medicine made from the bark of trees. Soon after, she went to work in the cloud forests of Costa Rica, Central America, where she ended up spending about 40 years climbing trees to study the canopy.

The canopy of a rainforest is one of the richest places for life. It's where about half of the world's animals and plants live because it's so light, sheltered and full of food. Nalini loved to study the **epiphytes**, the plants that grow on tree trunks and branches. The trees were very tall so she had to use a rope, harness, helmet and clips to climb safely. To get the climbing rope up a tree she'd attach it to a weighted fishing line, which was fired over a high branch with a slingshot. Nalini had learned modern dance as a teenager, a skill that made her more flexible for moving through the branches. Sometimes she'd even sleep in a hammock in the treetops. While in Costa Rica she met Jack, a scientist studying ants (there are about 4000 ant species that live only in the forest canopy). Nalini and Jack fell in love and they got married while perched 30 metres (100 feet) up a silk-cotton tree in the jungle.

Over the years in the rainforest Nalini realized that people tended to ignore trees, and she wondered how she could reconnect them. Since then, she's made it her life's work to bring people and trees together, especially through the arts. She has worked with rap artists to make tree-music, organized tree-dances, designed a tree logo for skateboards, and made a tree-climbing outfit for a Barbie doll. She's started projects that bring science and nature to people in prisons. For one project she worked with prisoners to grow mosses that were endangered in old forests. *TIME* magazine named her prison work as one the best ideas of the year. Nalini also talks in churches, synagogues and temples about how trees have inspired people in all religions.

One reason it's easy to ignore trees is that they seem like statues. Nalini wanted to show how much trees actually move, so she helped a tree to paint a picture. She tied a paintbrush to the tip of a branch, dipped it in green paint, and held up a piece of paper. As the wind moved the branch, the tree painted a picture that looked like ancient handwriting. By measuring the painted lines she worked out that the tree's branches moved over 300,000 kilometres (186,474 miles) in a year.

Nalini believes it's important to be thankful for trees because they do so much for us: they clean the air we breathe and fight climate change by soaking up CO_2. Trees meet many other human needs too, giving us food, shelter and places to enjoy. She says that when people realize the value of trees they will want to protect them:

'What keeps me hopeful is my sense that trees are deeply connected to humans, and humans are deeply connected to trees.'

Find out more

Nalini Nadkarni: https://nalininadkarni.com/

Spirit of the forest

Trees in human culture

We humans have always felt close to trees because they've helped us throughout our history. Our early ancestors spent 80 million years living in forests as they evolved into us. One reason we developed thumbs on our hands is to grab branches (no wonder we still love climbing trees). Most cultures have tree celebrations, beliefs and myths about how trees connect people to an unseen world.

The ancient Greeks believed each tree had its own spirit (a 'dryad') who lived within it and cared for the tree. Knocking on the trunk was like asking the tree spirit for help, and many people today still touch wood for good luck. Trees were valued for firewood, building, food and medicine, so people in the past believed they were supernatural helpers. They knew that if they looked after the trees, they'd get good rains and food crops (this is true, because trees recycle water and enrich the soil). Tree have always fired our imagination, from the dark forests in Grimms' fairytales to the magical lights of Christmas trees.

Tree of knowing

One of the oldest stories is about a tree that grew in the garden of the first human beings. Adam and Eve are warned not to eat an apple from the 'Tree of the Knowledge of Good and Evil' or they'll suddenly know too much — but being curious humans, they can't keep their hands off the fruit.

The apple tree later inspired one of the greatest pieces of science knowledge. The story goes that a young scientist named Isaac Newton was having a cup of tea and daydreaming under his apple tree in 1666. He saw an apple fall from the

The woods are lovely, dark and deep
—Robert Frost (1923)

tree and realized that this was due to the same force (gravity) that pulled the moon towards Earth. His apple tree is still alive in England. Today, apples are one of the most popular fruits in the world with over 7000 different kinds.

Protector tree

The bark of the birch tree has dark spots that look a bit like eyes, so it's been called 'The Watcher'. Many ancient people believed that the birch protected them from harm. The Celts saw the tree as a goddess who kept them safe, so they used the wood for brooms to sweep away bad spirits. Native American tribes used parts of the birch tree to make medicines, and built canoes from the waterproof bark.

Science also tells us that birch trees are strong protectors. The leaves remove pollution from the air, so the trees are often planted beside smelly motorways. Birch bark contains a chemical that protects the tree from pests. And those dark eye-spots are actually thickened bark that defends the tree from fire.

Sweetest tree

The sugar maple gives us one of the most delicious tree-treats: maple syrup. The Algonquin tribes of North America considered the tree a gift from the Great Spirit. They ate the sweet sap and also got medicines from the tree. An old Algonquin legend says that very thick sap once flowed from the tree. One day the hero Manbozho visited a village and found the people lying under the trees. They lay back with their mouths open and the thick sap dripped in. Manbozho was angered by their laziness, so he poured water into the tree to dilute the sap ... and ever since, people have had to boil the sap for ages to thicken it into syrup (40 parts sap boils down to make 1 part syrup). Scientists have now shown that maple syrup has chemicals that can fight disease in humans.

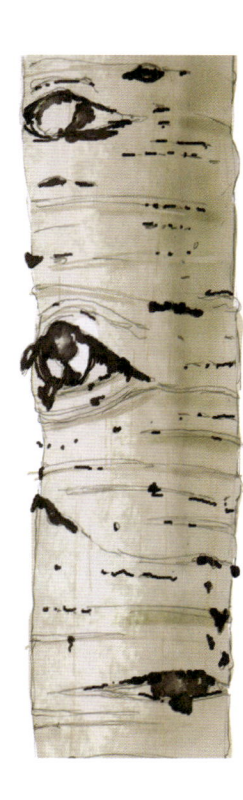

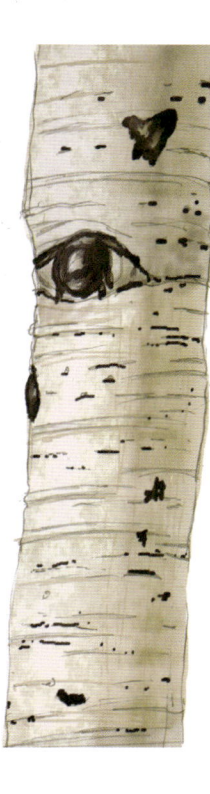

Tapping a maple does not harm the tree if it's done carefully.

These trees shall be my books.
—William Shakespeare, *As You Like It* (1599)

Universe tree

In Norse mythology a mighty ash tree called Yggdrasil is at the centre of the universe, connecting the many worlds of the gods. A wise eagle guards the top of the tree and deep underground the evil Nidhog is forever trying to destroy the roots. The Norse gods carved the first man (named Ask) from an ash tree, and the first woman (Embla) from an elm tree. The mighty god Thor made his spear from ash wood, and in real life the Vikings made weapons and oars from it.

In England the ash tree was thought to have healing powers and a sick child would be passed between the branches of the tree.

Tree of Life

The yew tree has been called the tree of life and death. Death, because the toxic seeds, leaves and bark can kill if eaten. Life,

The English longbow was about 1.8 metres (6 feet) long.

because yew trees can live for thousands of years and the wood is slow to rot. The world's oldest known wooden tool is a spear tip made of yew — the hunting weapon is over 300,000 years old! Yew wood is hard but bendy, so it was used to make longbows in the Middle Ages, the time of Robin Hood. Yews were sacred trees in the United Kingdom and were often planted by churches. A yew tree still alive in a churchyard in Llangernyw, Wales, is about 4000 years old. Today the yew is again seen as a tree of life because its powerful chemicals are made into an anti-cancer medicine.

God of the forest

The New Zealand kauri trees are the biggest rainforest trees in the world. The Māori people tell a creation story about the god Tāne pushing his parents apart to separate the earth and the sky. Then Tāne covered the land in his children, the trees and plants. Kauri trees are so tall and massive, they're said to be the legs of Tāne, holding up the sky. The most famous kauri is named Tāne Mahuta, meaning 'god of the forest'. It's 50 metres (164 feet) tall, almost 2000 years old, and looks big enough to stop the sky falling. Kauri trees are great at storing carbon from the air, so they're helping to shelter the Earth from the dangers of climate change.

72

BIG IDEA 4

trees
need
our help

Saving the oldest forest

John Seed

They faced bulldozers and made a human forest in a battle to save the oldest rainforest in the world.

John Seed lived near a beautiful rainforest in Australia but he knew very little about it until some neighbours asked him for help. They were going to protest against the cutting of the rainforest trees and John said he'd join them. His decision to help save the forest would turn his life around.

People had tried for years to stop the government cutting down trees in Terania Creek rainforest in New South Wales, Australia. In 1979 they decided that **people power** was the only way left to protest. John joined a camp of about 300 peaceful protestors who'd blocked roads into the forest. When the logging workers arrived with a bulldozer, the protesters were in their way. John and the others sang 'All we are saying, is give trees a chance'. The protestors talked the loggers into leaving, but the next day the bulldozer returned with a guard of 100 armed police. This time the police dragged the singing protesters out of the way and arrested many of them. The action was reported on TV and in newspapers.

For the next few days bulldozers cleared a road into the forest while a swarm of protestors tried to block their path. The chainsawing of trees began and the

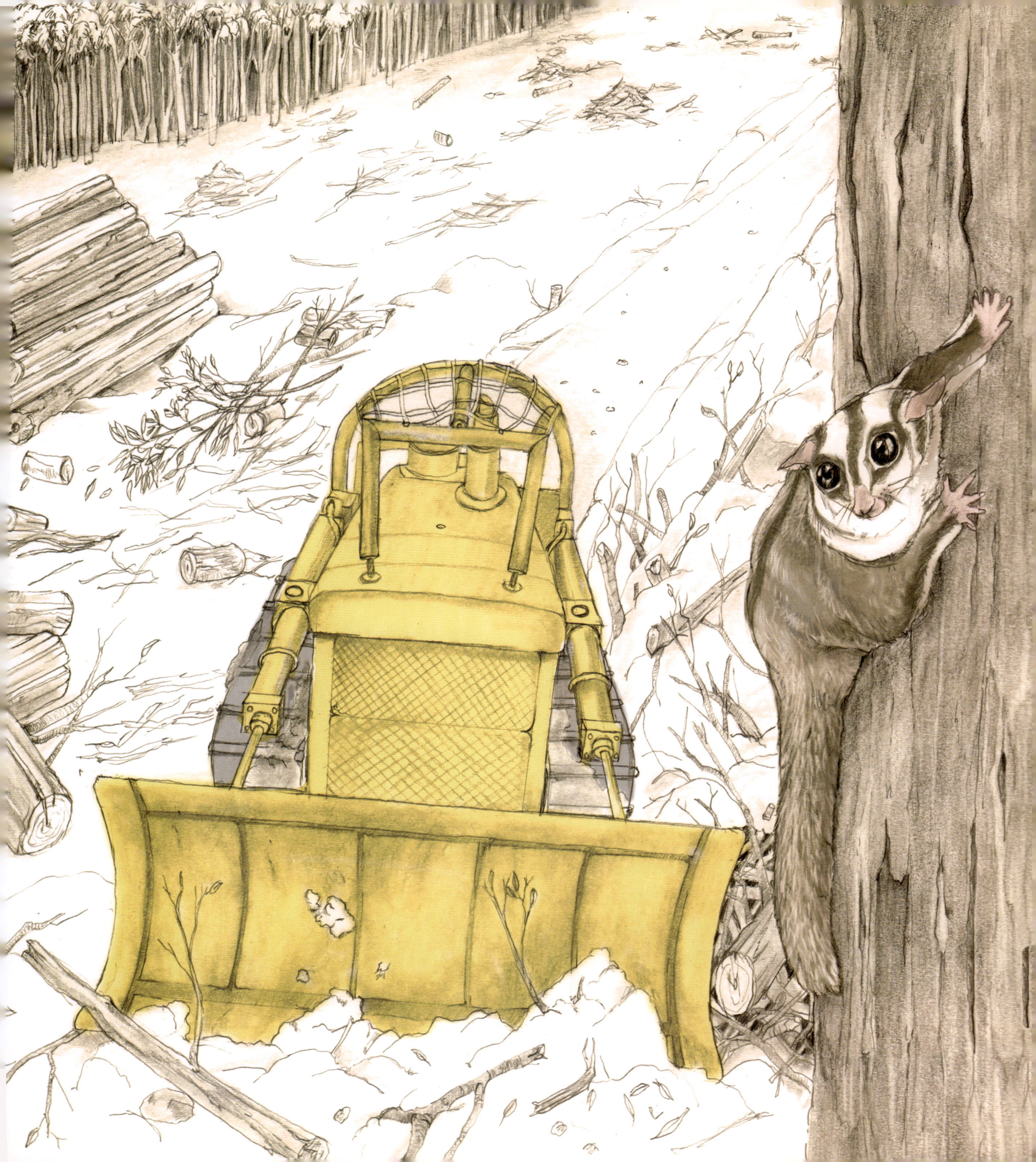

The story of brazil nuts

The brazil nut tree has a special partnership with two small rainforest creatures. The tall tree needs its flowers pollinated so it can make nuts — this is the job of the orchid bee. It's the only bee strong enough to crawl inside the tough brazil flowers. The other partner is a small mammal called an agouti. Brazil nuts grow inside a hard wooden case the size of a baseball, but the agouti's teeth are strong enough to crack it open. The agouti buries the nuts to eat later, but a few will sprout into new trees. Almost all the brazil nuts we eat come from trees growing in wild rainforests, because that's where the bee and the agouti live.

police took protestors away. John and the others did all they could to peacefully stop the destruction: they climbed the trees, stood in front of the bulldozers, and sang songs. But it was a dangerous place to be with trees falling all around them. Messages of support came from all over Australia as the tree-cutting went on. At last the government was forced to stop the logging of the precious rainforest. Talking about the Terania forest protest, John says,

'Something happened there which I can't really explain, that changed the direction of my life ... I heard the trees screaming. I heard them calling to us for help and I couldn't resist that call.'

After that, John joined in more protests around Australia to stop the killing of other rainforests. One of the biggest was in Tasmania in 1982, where a dam was to be built which would flood the rainforest. Thousands protested and the forest was saved. But when they tried to stop the logging of the Daintree rainforest in Queensland a year later, they found that the news media had lost interest in reporting about tree protests.

The Daintree rainforest is like a living museum. It's been there for 180 million years, making it the oldest rainforest on the planet. It is home to some incredible life, including 80 per cent of the world's fern species, and a huge range of Australia's birds, reptiles, mammals and insects. John and a group of protestors had to find a way to get the Daintree into the news and let everyone know it was under attack. Their plan was to stop a logging road being bulldozed into the forest.

On a narrow part of the road some of them buried themselves up to their chests in the ground. There was no way for the bulldozers to get past this forest of humans. The police arrived and removed the group using diggers with heavy metal scoops. Their dramatic protest made the news but it took a few more years of protests to save the Daintree rainforest. It's now fully protected.

Over time John learned that rainforests are important for the health of the living planet. Trees enrich the air, rainfall, soil and wildlife habitats. But he also saw how quickly they were being destroyed, so he started the Rainforest Information Centre to sound the alarm. John has worked to protect and plant rainforests in many countries, and was awarded the Order of Australia Medal for his efforts. He says that we can easily forget that humans are a part of nature:

'We are like a leaf believing itself to be separate from the tree on which it grows.'

Just imagine a leaf trying to destroy the tree it grows upon! If humans are to survive we must look after the natural world.

Find out more

Rainforest Information Centre:
www.rainforestinformationcentre.org

Green warriors of the Earth

The toughest trees

The word 'tree' comes from the ancient word 'deru' which means solid, faithful and long-lasting (it's also where we get the word 'true'). Trees have evolved amazing ways to grow in extreme places, from mountains to deserts, in burning heat and freezing cold, and even in sea water!

Here are some of the toughest trees on the planet.

Scuba tree

Mangrove trees grow in sea water on the coast. The tree has many tricks to survive, including holding its breath underwater! The roots have breathing holes that open when the tide goes out and close up when it returns; and mangroves can take the salt out of sea water.

Mangrove seeds grow into baby trees while still perching on their parents' branches above the water, then drop into the mud where they quickly put down roots. The long roots are like stilts, standing strong in the waves.

Mangroves are important trees because they shelter sea creatures, protect us from floods and fight climate change. Mangroves can suck in four times more carbon than other trees. There are forests of mangroves around Florida, United States.

Fire tree

Crush a leaf from a gum tree (eucalyptus) and sniff the fresh scent. The oil in the leaf is 'volatile', meaning it quickly travels into the air. It's found in all parts of the tree and it can burn like crazy. What's more, the tree's dry bark and leaves are the perfect fire-starter. A gum tree is a firebomb waiting to explode.

So how does it survive in sizzling hot Australia? Gum trees use fire. The faster a fire races past, the more likely they will survive, so they make the fire speed up. Their oil ignites in jets of flame, while bark and leaves burn in a flash. The fire moves on, leaving smooth trunks that can now sprout new branches. Gums also grow well after fires: the seed capsules open up when cooked, and ash feeds the new trees.

Indigenous Australians used gum trees to make canoes, boomerangs and medicines. Eucalyptus oil can fight bacteria and is used to ease coughs and colds. The strangest gum-fact of all is that the roots can bring up gold particles from underground, and the gold ends up in the leaves.

Dynamite tree

The sandbox tree is not for hugging. It's nicknamed the 'dynamite tree' because the seed pod is like a time bomb. The pod dries out and one hot day suddenly explodes, shooting out seeds out at about 240 kilometres per hour (150 mph). The trunk is covered in fearsome spikes, so in tropical countries it's called the 'monkey no-climb' tree. Worse still, most parts of the tree are poisonous if eaten, and the sap can cause blindness. Why does it have all these deadly weapons? To protect itself. Trees can't run away from pests and must defend themselves with a tough skin and chemicals.

Lava tree

The New Zealand pōhutukawa can live to be over 1000 years old. It's tough enough to survive fierce storms and grow in difficult places such as volcanoes. Pōhutukawa roots can grow through the air and anchor into rocks, even on a cliff-face. The species that grows in Hawaii is often the first tree to grow after a volcano erupts and the lava cools. The largest pōhutukawa forest in the world grows on old lava on Rangitoto Island, New Zealand. It's called the Iron Tree because the wood is so strong — New Zealand Māori used it to make tools, paddles and weapons.

Super trees

The boreal forest is the toughest on Earth. It covers over half of Canada, and grows across Russia and Scandinavia, all the way to Scotland. It's like a great green headscarf tied around the top of the planet. The boreal trees can withstand temperatures from about -50°C (-122°F) in winter, up to 40°C (104°F) in summer. The forest holds many world records: it's the largest on Earth; it holds the most fresh water; and it's the biggest carbon store on land. The Canadian boreal forest hosts up to 3 billion songbirds, which fly there every year to nest.

THE SECRET OF TREE STRENGTH

What makes a tree so strong? The secret is that the trunk has many layers inside it, each one with a special job. From the outside, the layers are:

- a tough coat of **bark**
- a layer of tubes where food moves around the tree (**phloem**)
- a thin layer which is the growing part of the tree (**cambium**)
- the layer that water moves through (**xylem**)
- finally, the **heartwood**, which is dead wood. The heartwood is like a steel-hard skeleton which won't rot as long as it's inside the living tree. That's how a tree stays so strong while it grows ... it's alive and dead at the same time!

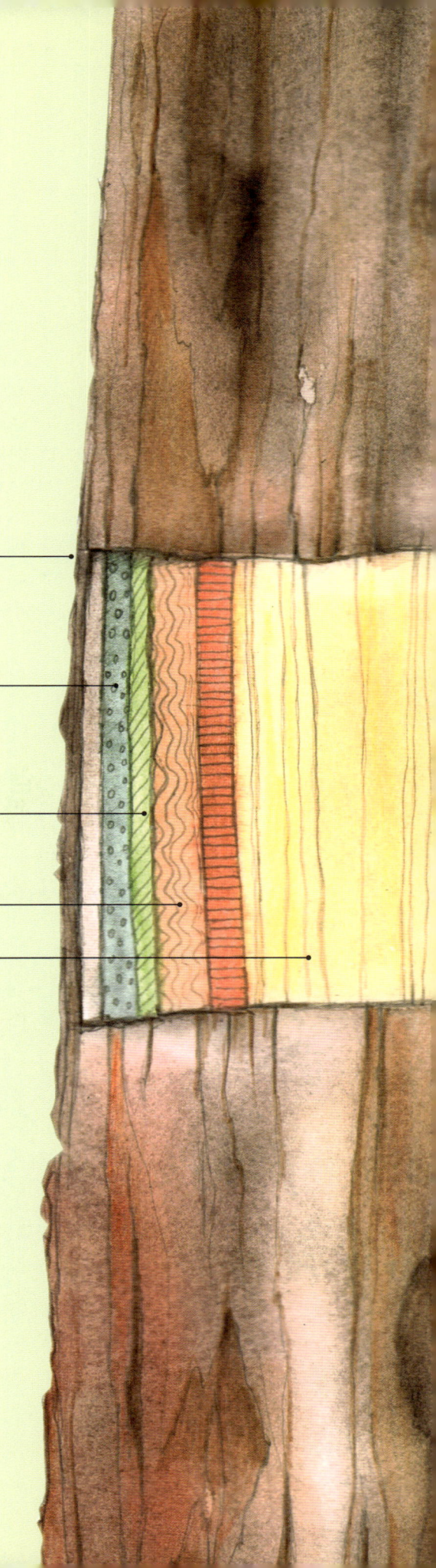

Letter from a tree

Dean Baigent-Mercer

Young people lived in the trees to save an ancient forest from being turned into toilet seats!

When Kiwi Dean Baigent-Mercer was in his early twenties, a friend told him that the New Zealand government was cutting down ancient rainforest trees. At first he didn't believe it. He knew that over half of the country's **native forests** had been destroyed in the past. Surely people knew better in 1996!

'I was aware of climate change and the importance of trees as the greatest living capture of carbon, as well as being the lungs of the planet. We'd lost so much forest already, we couldn't afford to lose any more.'

The trees were also home to endangered animals such as the kiwi. Dean joined a group of young protestors at Charleston Forest where the logging had started. They planned to live among the rimu (red pine) trees to let all New Zealanders know about it.

The group entered the forest one wet night to get close to the cutting area. They put up tents and hid from the loggers for a few days. Meanwhile, helicopters flew overhead carrying rimu trunks, on their way to the timber mill. Some of the trees had been there longer than humans had been in New Zealand, but were now being made into products such as toilet seats.

Imagine you are there on that day in 1997 ...

The loggers have gone home after a day's work and the forest is at peace again. The young protesters come out of hiding and head towards the cutting site. But what's that weird smell? They emerge into a clearing and are shocked by the wasteland ahead — decapitated tops of big rimu trees that have crashed to the ground; severed trunks lying on a tangle of smaller trees and crushed ferns. It's as if a missile has hit. They realize that the pungent smell is the sap bleeding from the cut trees.

What took hundreds of years to grow is now smashed. But the forest that still stands can be saved. The protesters clamber across the mess. They tie white ribbons around the old rimu trunks that are next in line for the chop and put up these signs:

FOREST OCCUPIED!

Trees tied with white ribbons mark some of the areas of forest being occupied by people who believe these native forests should not be logged.

That evening Dean tries to get comfortable in his tent but it's not easy on the sloping ground covered in roots. He finally gets to sleep but is woken by a sound like a firehose blasting his tent. The rain has returned.

After a sleepless night, a few protestors meet the loggers arriving in the morning. They give each of the workers a box of chocolates, saying, 'This protest isn't against you personally, it's against the government logging.'

The men keep working, but before long, word of the forest occupation makes it into the national news.

One of their protest actions was tree-sitting. Some branches were five storeys up, and during one climb up, Dean slipped off a mossy branch and fell 2 metres (6 feet) before his safety harness stopped him. Another time he was pulling himself up onto a branch and plunged his hand into a live wasp's nest.

Dean and the others soon got to know the forest as if it was their own neighbourhood. There was one spectacular rimu that became Dean's favourite tree to climb. One day he wrote this letter to his family:

Dear Ma, Pa and Ja

Guess where I am? I'm clipped on to a branch, while sitting on a small platform with my friend Jen. We're probably 30 metres (100 feet) above the forest floor. This is my 22nd day here and I'm loving it. There are birds fluttering about and cicadas are singing their hearts out. When there's a breeze the crown of this rimu sways and it feels like a fairground ride. Surprisingly I'm not scared ... maybe this is because this is one of the most important and courageous things I've ever done.

It's so beautiful here with the trees we climb and shelter under, carpets of fern, kiwi that shriek at night, and the river where we wash and drink. This is what I've grown to appreciate and this is exactly what the logging destroys. It's paradise here and I'm more determined than ever it stays that way.

Lots of love from the rainforest canopy.

Dean

'I looked up after writing that letter and a bright-green parakeet shot over my head and dipped right in front of me. It was as if it was thanking us for saving its home.'

The Charleston Forest occupation goes down as a legend of non-violent action in New Zealand.

—Helen Clark, former Head of the United Nations Development Program and NZ Prime Minister

The group lived in the forest for five months. As they watched the logs being taken away, it sometimes felt like nothing could stop it. But many people now knew about the logging, and protests sprang up around New Zealand. People wrote thousands of letters to the government demanding an end to the destruction. The government stopped the logging and one of the last old rainforests in New Zealand was saved.

The tree which moves some to tears of Joy, is in the Eyes of others only a Green thing that stands in their way.

—William Blake (1799)

Find out more

Forest and Bird: https://www.forestandbird.org.nz/

86

Chipko!

The first tree huggers

Women hugged trees to save their forests from being cut down.

A protest by Indian women started a tree-hugging movement around the planet. It all began in the Himalayan forests of northern India in the 1970s. The heavy monsoon rains brought deadly floods and landslides, damaging villages in poor communities. The villagers knew that the soil had been washed away because too many trees had been cut down. The roots had held the soil in place and also soaked up the rain. People started a new kind of protest called 'Chipko', which means 'to hug'.

The government was about to cut a forest near the village of Reni. The village men protested but the government used a tricky plan to get rid of the them. They paid the men to go to a meeting in another village. When the men had gone, the loggers moved into their forest to begin cutting.

The Reni forest was saved and the area later became a national park. This tree-hugging protest was a big step forward for Indian women because men usually took the lead. The protest idea spread quickly and led to a ban on cutting trees in the Himalayas.

'Chipko!' became the cry to save forests all over India. One big protest was in Magaddi Forest in 1978, where 3000 people, one for every tree, stood guard day

Imagine you are there on that day in 1974 …

It's early morning and the pine forest is still quite dark. Young Vimla is gathering dry sticks for a fire. As she wanders around the edge of the forest, her mother's words come back to her: 'Don't go into the forest alone. It's not safe for young girls with all these protests happening.'

But Vimla isn't scared, the trees are her friends. She hears men's voices coming from the dim forest. *That's strange, she thinks. The village men are all away. Who could it be?* Vimla darts from tree to tree to get a look. There they are, walking through the forest, carrying saws and axes. The logging men! She must tell someone.

Vimla sprints like the wind back to the village, straight to Gaura Devi's house. Gauri leads the Women's Club — she'll know what to do. Vimla runs inside, breathless.

'The logging men … attacking the forest … what can we do?'

Gaura acts quickly.

'Vimla, run to every house and tell the women to meet me here. Quick now!'

Within the hour, a group of 30 women are marching into the forest. Vimla is allowed to go with them. They reach the loggers, who are preparing to cut into the trees.

'Chipko!' shouts Gaura, and groups of women surround the nearby trees, holding hands around the trunks.

'Go home so we can do our jobs,' says the leader of the loggers.

'No,' says Gaura. 'This forest has always been our home. We will protect it with our bodies.'

The loggers talk among themselves. They decide they don't want the women to get hurt, so they leave the forest.

But the villagers stay on to guard the trees.

and night until it was saved. It was a community celebration with children and musicians. Here's one of the Chipko songs:

What does the forest bear? Soil, water and pure air, soil, water and pure air, the basis of our life.

Today, tree planting is highly valued by India in its efforts to fight climate change. It has a world record of over 50 million trees planted in just one day in northern India, not far from where Chipko started.

The Chipko tree huggers have inspired protesters all over the world. 'Tree hugger' has often been used as a put-down, to mean that people were too soft-hearted about nature. But the tree huggers have been proved right: trees are like a green skin defending the planet. We humans are a part of nature too, so it would be stupid not to care for it.

Trees look after us ... let's look after trees.

Clean as a neem

The neem tree in India is one of the most helpful trees in the world. For thousands of years people have made medicines from all parts of the neem — the chemicals in the tree can fight viruses, bacteria and fungi. Its leaves, bark, seeds and oil contain a powerful insect repellent — but not the flowers, because the tree needs bees. Indians put the leaves in their cupboards to keep food safe from insects, and neem trees are planted beside hospitals and homes. Neem is used around the world to help control garden pests.

What can you do?

Each one of us can do something to help trees — even the smallest action will make a difference to the planet.

Plant a tree — it's one of the best ways to fight climate change.

Protest against the cutting of old native forests — they're the best trees at storing CO_2.

Recycle paper and wood products.

May the forest be with you!

Glossary
Science words explained

Aerial roots Roots that grow above ground, from branches or trunks

Carbon A common chemical found in all living things

Carbon dioxide (CO$_2$) A gas in the air; animals breathe it out

Carbon store Where carbon is stored in nature (e.g. in trees, coal, oil, gas)

Climate change Warming of the planet's atmosphere caused by humans

Conservation Caring for and healing the living planet

Ecosystem A natural community of living things and their surrounding habitat

Epiphyte A plant that grows on another plant (e.g. ferns, mosses, orchids)

Habitat An area in nature that is the home neighbourhood of an animal

Inanimate Showing no signs of life

Logging Cutting down trees to use the wood or to clear the land

Native forest The original plants that first grew in a place

Oxygen (O$_2$) A gas in the air; animals need it to stay alive

People power Non-violent protest by large groups of people

Photosynthesis How plants make food for themselves; 'photo' means light, and 'synthesis' means building

Pollination Transfer of pollen that helps trees make seeds, nuts and fruit

Seedling A young tree

Species A group of very similar living things

Wood-wide-web Underground web of fungi connecting tree roots in a forest

References

Where do the quotes come from?

Page 24, Jane Goodall quotes: *Seeds of Hope* by Jane Goodall and Gail Hudson, 2014, Hachette Book Group.

Page 37 Wangari Maathai quotes: 'Wangari Maathai Nobel Peace Prize speech', © The Nobel Foundation.

Pages 39–41, 47, Richard St. Barbe Baker quotes: *My Life – My Trees* by Richard St. Barbe Baker, 1970, Lutterworth Press

Pages 45, 47, Felix Finkbeiner quotes: Plant-for-the-Planet

Pages 60–61, Suzanne Simard quotes: www.TED.com, 'How trees talk to each other', 2016

Pages 64, 67, Nalini Nadkarni quotes: www.treestoryfilm.com, 'Nalini Nadkarni: Dancer in the Canopy', 2016, Woody Creek Pictures.

Page 77, John Seed quotes: author interview, 2018

Pages 82, 84, Dean Baigent-Mercer quotes: author interview, 2018.

Page 63, *Science and Spiritual Practices* by Rupert Sheldrake, 2018, Hodder & Stoughton.

Other references

Unbowed by Wangari Maathai, 2007, Heinemann.

The Hidden Life of Trees by Peter Wohlleben, 2017, HarperCollins Publishers.

What Has Nature Ever Done for Us? by Tony Juniper, 2013, Profile Books.

The Legacy of Luna by Julia Butterfly Hill, 2000, HarperCollins Publishers.

Acknowledgments

Many thanks to:

The University of Otago College of Education and Creative New Zealand.

Dr Jane Goodall and Dr Melanie Vivian of the Jane Goodall Institute.

Dean Baigent-Mercer, John Seed, and Ann Marie Barnes.

John Steel, Botany Dept, Otago University.

Tree Beings summarizes people's lives — some events are dramatized and are the author's own interpretation.

Puzzles & Mazes

🌀 **Can you find these 70 creatures hidden in the tree on the front cover?**

ant	cricket	gecko	man	seahorse
baby	crocodile	giraffe	monkey	seal
bat	crab	goat	moose	starfish
bear	deer	grub	moth	shark
beaver	dog	gorilla	mouse	sheep
bee	dolphin	hippo	ostrich	sloth
beetle	dove	horse	otter	snail
buffalo	dragonfly	kangaroo	owl	snake
butterfly	duck	kiwi	penguin	spider
camel	echidna	koala	pig	squirrel
cardinal	elephant	ladybird	rabbit	stingray
cat	emu	leopard	raven	tortoise
chicken	fox	lion	rhino	whale
cow	frog	llama	scorpion	woman

🌀 **And these creatures are hidden in the illustration on page 2!**

baby	crocodile	goat	moth	sheep
bat	deer	gorilla	mouse	sloth
bear	dog	hippo	ostrich	snail
beaver	dolphin	horse	otter	snake
bee	dove	kangaroo	owl	spider
buffalo	dragonfly	kiwi	pig	squirrel
butterfly	echidna	koala	rabbit	stingray
camel	elephant	leopard	raven	tortoise
cardinal	emu	lion	rhino	whale
cat	fox	llama	seahorse	woman
chicken	frog	man	seal	
cow	gecko	monkey	starfish	
cricket	giraffe	moose	shark	

🌀 **Make sure you also explore the mazes inside the front and back covers of the book, and also on pages 90-91.**

🌀 **And did you spot the number hidden in the trees on pages 44-45?**

🌀 **How many insects can you find in the pictures inside the book?**

Index

A
Acacia trees 56
Adam and Eve 68
air quality 19-21
airborne scents, tree warning signal 56
apple trees 68

B
Baigent-Mercer, Dean 82-5
Baker, Richard St. Barbe 38-41
banyan tree, widest tree 28
Beech (Jane's tree friend) 24
Beni forest 88
biggest tree 28
birch tree bark 69
boreal forests 81
brazil nuts 76
bristlecone pine, oldest tree 28

C
Caledonian forest, saving 46
Canadian forests 61
carbon dioxide (CO_2) 19, 20, 42, 45, 46
Charleston Forest (NZ) 82-5
chimpanzee (David) 26
Chinese proverb, tree planting 43
Chipko tree huggers 87-9
climate change 20, 45

D
Daintree rainforest 77
Dance of the Trees 39-40
David (chimpanzee) 26
dead trees, bursting with life 21
'dryad' (tree spirit) 68
dynamite tree 80

E
epiphytes 66, 67

F
farmland, tree clearance 50-1
fig trees 33, 36
Finkbeiner, Felix 44-7
fire tree 80
'forest bathing', Japan 41
forests
    benefits of 41
    underground 60
fungi, tree roots network 57, 59-61

G
Gombe rainforest 24-5
Goodall, Dr Jane
    befriends trees 24-7
    living with wildlife 26-7
    message from 10-11
gravity 69
Green Belt Movement, Kenya 34-5, 37
grizzly bear 60
gum (eucalyptus) tree 80

H
Hill, Julia Butterfly 14-17
Himalayan forests 87
Hyperion (redwood tree) 29, 28

I
Iron Tree 81

J
Jigs (dog) 58-9

K
kauri creation story 71
kauri trees (NZ) 71

Kenya
    anti Green Belt 37
    Baker, Richard St. Barbe 39-40
    tree planting 34-5, 37

L
lava tree 80-1
letter from a tree 84
logging
    California 14-17
    Charleston Forest (NZ) 82-5
    Daintree 77
    India 87-9
    Tarania Creek 74
    see also protestors
longbow, English 70
Luna (redwood tree) 14-17

M
Maathai, Professor Wangari 32-7
Magaddi Forest 88
mangrove trees 79-80
medicines, from trees 64, 67
Men of the Trees, Kenya 40
messages, between trees 55, 56
mother trees 57

N
Nadkarni, Professor Nalini 64-7

neem tree 89
Newton Isaac 68
Norse mythology, Yggdrasil (tree) 70

O
oldest tree 28

P
painted picture by a tree 67
photosynthesis 19
Plant-for-the-Planet group 46–7
planting, ways to do it 42
pōhutakawa tree 80–1
protector tree 69
protestors
    attacked 34, 37
    Charleston Forest (NZ) 82–5
    removed 74, 77
    tree huggers 87–9
    using forest nicknames 14

R
rain, trees' contribution 20, 25
rainforests
    as a habitat 66, 67, 77
    logging protests 74, 77
    power of 25
    see also logging
reconnection with trees 67
redwood trees
    biggest 28
    felling 16–17
    history of 17
    tallest 28, 29
    under threat 14
regrowth, benefit for farmers 50–1
rimu (red pine) trees 82–5
Rinaudo, Tony 49–51
Root & Shoots club 27

S
sandbox tree 80
Scotland, native forests 46
scuba tree 79–80
Seed, John 74, 77
Simard, Professor Suzanne 58–61
soil, tree roots care for 20–1
sugar maple sap legend 69
sunlight 19
sweetest tree 69

T
tallest tree 28, 29
Tarania Creek rainforest 74
TED Talk, Simard's 61
toilet pit, dog in 58–9
tree, meaning of the word 79
tree clearance 50–1
tree huggers, first 87–9
tree nurseries, destroyed 37, 39
tree of life and death 70–1
tree planters, attacked 34, 37
tree rings 56
tree roots, underground network 57, 59–61
tree sitting 83
treehouse, boat-shaped 64, 65
tree-planting dance 39–40

trees
    easy to ignore 54
    in everyday language 61
    layers of trunks 81
    making friends with 24–7, 62–3
    smart senses 57
    strength 81
    value of 67, 68
    why they are vital 57
tree-sitting 14, 16–17

W
wasps, fig trees need 36
water, trees use of 20
websites
    Baker documentary 41
    Circle of Life 17
    Forest and Bird 85
    Green Belt Movement 37
    Help Plant Trees 42
    International Tree Foundation 41
    Men of the Trees 41
    Nalini Nadkarni 67
    Plant-for-the-Planet 47
    Rainforest Information Centre 77
    Right Livelihood award 51
    Roots & Shoots 27
    Simard's TED Talk 61
widest tree 28
wildlife
    Jane living with 26–7
    in trees 21
wood-wide internet 61
world record trees 28

Y
yew tree 70–1

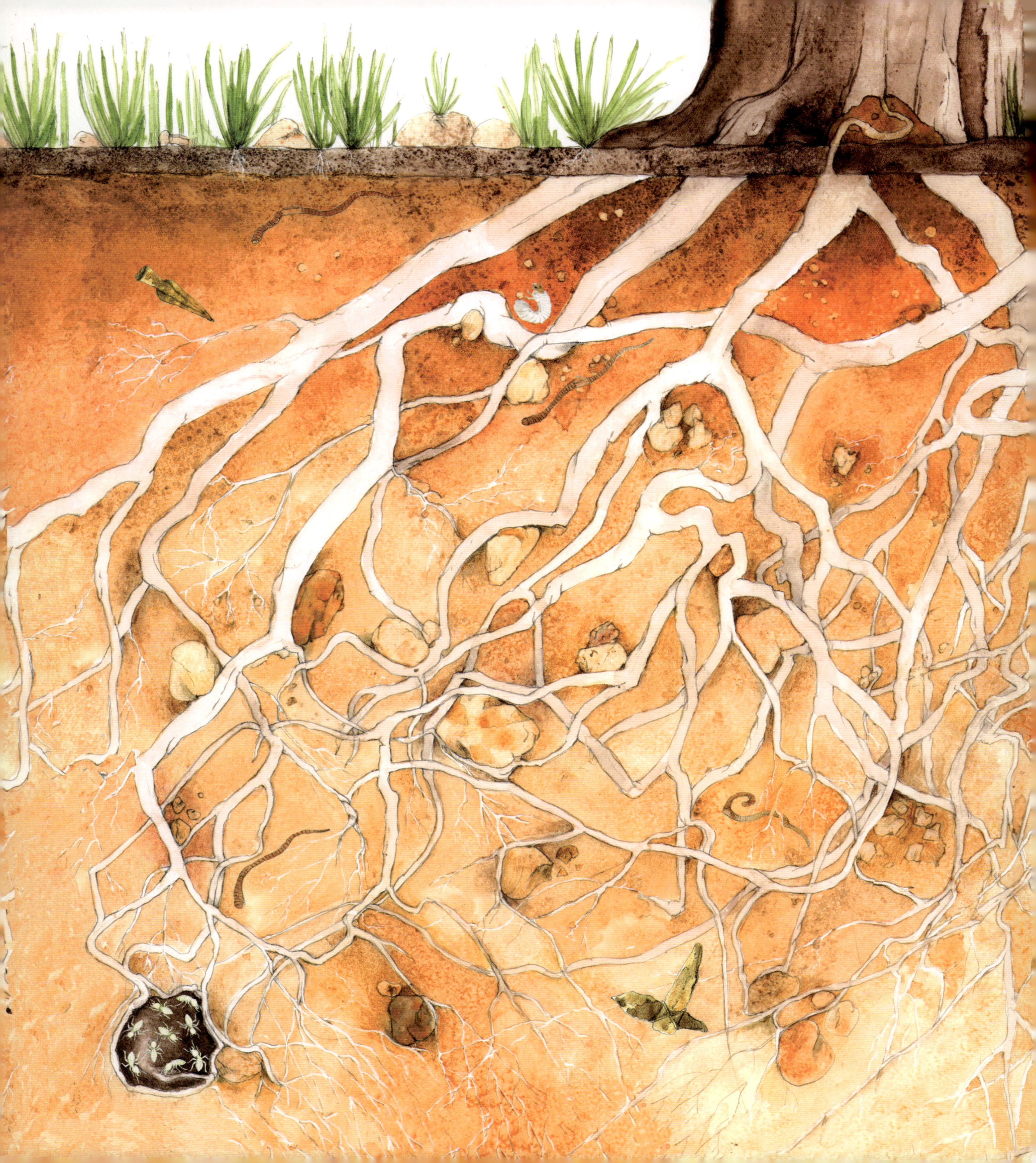